This book belongs to...

_____

About Me

My birthday is _____

I am _____ years old.

I live in _____

all of my favorites...

animal: _____

book: _____

color: _____

dessert: _____

food: _____

movie: _____

place to visit: _____

season: _____

song: _____

sport: _____

toy: _____

TV show: _____

This is a drawing of me...

date: _____

Today I feel...

😁 🙂 😐 🙁 😠 😛 😮 😖

I am grateful for

1. _____

2. _____

3. _____

Something that made me smile today...

_____

This is the best thing that happened to me today...

date: _____

Today I feel...

😁 🙂 😐 🙁 😠 😛 😲 😖

I am grateful for

1. _____

2. _____

3. _____

Today I learned...

_____

This is the best thing that happened to me today...

date: _____

Today I feel...

😁 🙂 😐 🙁 😠 😛 😲 😖

I am grateful for

1. _____

2. _____

3. _____

This person made me happy today...

_____

This is the best thing that happened to me today...

date: _____

Today I feel...

😄 🙂 😐 🙁 😠 😛 😲 😖

I am grateful for

1. _____

2. _____

3. _____

This is what I am looking forward to next week...

_____

This is the best thing that happened to me today...

date: _____

Today I feel...

😁 🙂 😐 🙁 😠 😛 😲 😟

I am grateful for

1. _____

2. _____

3. _____

This is one nice thing I did for someone today...

_____

This is the best thing that happened to me today...

Laughing Out Loud!

These are the things that make me
laugh hysterically!

1. _____

2. _____

3. _____

This is a drawing of something that makes me laugh
out loud...

date: _____

Today I feel...

😁 🙂 😐 🙁 😠 😛 😮 😣

I am grateful for

1. _____

2. _____

3. _____

Something that made me smile today...

_____

This is the best thing that happened to me today...

Today I feel...

😄 🙂 😐 🙁 😠 😛 😮 😖

I am grateful for

1. _____

2. _____

3. _____

Today I learned...

_____

This is the best thing that happened to me today...

Today I feel...

😁 🙂 😐 ☹️ 😣 😛 😲 😖

I am grateful for

1. _____

2. _____

3. _____

This person made me happy today...

_____

This is the best thing that happened to me today...

date: _____

Today I feel...

😁 😊 😐 🙁 😠 😛 😮 😖

I am grateful for

1. _____

2. _____

3. _____

This is what I am looking forward to next week...

_____

This is the best thing that happened to me today...

date: _____

Today I feel...

😄 🙂 😐 🙁 😠 😛 😯 😖

I am grateful for

1. _____

2. _____

3. _____

This is one nice thing I did for someone today...

_____

This is the best thing that happened to me today...

I can do anything I put my mind to!

When I grow up I want to be...

date: _____

Today I feel...

😁 🙂 😐 ☹️ 😠 😝 😮 😖

I am grateful for

1. _____

2. _____

3. _____

Something that made me smile today...

_____

This is the best thing that happened to me today...

date: _____

Today I feel...

😁 ☺️ 😐 🙁 😣 😛 😮 😖

I am grateful for

1. _____

2. _____

3. _____

Today I learned...

_____

This is the best thing that happened to me today...

date: _____

Today I feel...

😁 🙂 😐 🙁 😠 😛 😮 😖

I am grateful for

1. _____

2. _____

3. _____

This person made me happy today...

_____

This is the best thing that happened to me today...

date: _____

Today I feel...

😁 🙂 😐 🙁 😣 😛 😮 😖

I am grateful for

1. _____

2. _____

3. _____

This is what I am looking forward to next week...

_____

This is the best thing that happened to me today...

date: _____

Today I feel...

😃 🙂 😐 🙁 😠 😛 😲 😖

I am grateful for

1. _____

2. _____

3. _____

This is one nice thing I did for someone today...

_____

This is the best thing that happened to me today...

These are a few of my favorite things!

Below I circled all of the things I am thankful for...

date: _____

Today I feel...

😁 🙂 😐 🙁 😠 😛 😮 😰

I am grateful for

1. _____

2. _____

3. _____

Something that made me smile today...

_____

This is the best thing that happened to me today...

date: _____

Today I feel...

😁 🙂 😐 🙁 😠 😝 😲 😖

I am grateful for

1. _____

2. _____

3. _____

Today I learned...

_____

This is the best thing that happened to me today...

date: _____

Today I feel...

😁 🙂 😐 🙁 😠 😛 😲 😖

I am grateful for

1. _____

2. _____

3. _____

This person made me happy today...

_____

This is the best thing that happened to me today...

date: _____

Today I feel...

😁 🙂 😐 🙁 😠 😛 😮 😖

I am grateful for

1. _____

2. _____

3. _____

This is what I am looking forward to next week...

_____

This is the best thing that happened to me today...

date: _____

Today I feel...

😁 🙂 😐 🙁 😠 😛 😮 😰

I am grateful for

1. _____

2. _____

3. _____

This is one nice thing I did for someone today...

_____

This is the best thing that happened to me today...

One day I might feel down and that's ok.

I am allowed to feel scared, sad, or worried. When this happens some of the things that help me calm down or feel better are...

When others are scared, sad, or worried. I like to help them feel better by...

Today I feel...

😄 🙂 😐 🙁 😠 😛 😮 😖

I am grateful for

1. _____

2. _____

3. _____

Something that made me smile today...

_____

This is the best thing that happened to me today...

Today I feel...

😆 🙂 😐 🙁 😠 😛 😲 😰

I am grateful for

1. _____

2. _____

3. _____

Today I learned...

_____

This is the best thing that happened to me today...

date: _____

Today I feel...

😁 ☺ 😐 ☹ 😠 😛 😮 😖

I am grateful for

1. _____

2. _____

3. _____

This person made me happy today...

_____

This is the best thing that happened to me today...

Today I feel...

I am grateful for

1. _____

2. _____

3. _____

This is what I am looking forward to next week...

_____

This is the best thing that happened to me today...

date: _____

Today I feel...

😄　🙂　😐　🙁　😣　😛　😲　😖

I am grateful for

1. _____

2. _____

3. _____

This is one nice thing I did for someone today...

_____

This is the best thing that happened to me today...

I am awesome!

My friends and family would describe me as...

1. _____

2. _____

3. _____

What I like most about me is

_____

because _____

This is a drawing of my favorite thing about me...

date: _____

Today I feel...

😄 🙂 😐 🙁 😠 😛 😮 😟

I am grateful for

1. _____

2. _____

3. _____

Something that made me smile today...

_____

This is the best thing that happened to me today...

date: _____

Today I feel...

😁 🙂 😐 🙁 😠 😛 😮 😰

I am grateful for

1. _____

2. _____

3. _____

Today I learned...

_____

This is the best thing that happened to me today...

date: _____

Today I feel...

😆 ☺ 😐 🙁 😠 😛 😮 😖

I am grateful for

1. _____

2. _____

3. _____

This person made me happy today...

_____

This is the best thing that happened to me today...

date: _____

Today I feel...

😄 🙂 😐 🙁 😠 😛 😮 😟

I am grateful for

1. _____

2. _____

3. _____

This is what I am looking forward to next week...

_____

This is the best thing that happened to me today...

Today I feel...

😄 🙂 😐 🙁 😠 😝 😮 😖

I am grateful for

1. _____

2. _____

3. _____

This is one nice thing I did for someone today...

_____

This is the best thing that happened to me today...

Love the little things!

I can name things that I am thankful for that start with each of these letters...

G _____

R _____

A _____

T _____

E _____

F _____

U _____

L _____

date: _____

Today I feel...

😁 🙂 😐 🙁 😠 😛 😮 😖

I am grateful for

1. _____

2. _____

3. _____

Something that made me smile today...

_____

This is the best thing that happened to me today...

date: _____

Today I feel...

😄 🙂 😐 🙁 😠 😛 😮 😖

I am grateful for

1. _____

2. _____

3. _____

Today I learned...

_____

This is the best thing that happened to me today...

date: _____

Today I feel...

😁 🙂 😐 🙁 😠 😛 😮 😖

I am grateful for

1. _____

2. _____

3. _____

This person made me happy today...

_____

This is the best thing that happened to me today...

Today I feel...

😄 🙂 😐 🙁 😠 😛 😯 😰

I am grateful for

1. _____

2. _____

3. _____

This is what I am looking forward to next week...

_____

This is the best thing that happened to me today...

date: _____

Today I feel...

😁 😊 😐 ☹️ 😠 😛 😮 😵

I am grateful for

1. _____

2. _____

3. _____

This is one nice thing I did for someone today...

_____

This is the best thing that happened to me today...

My family loves me to the moon and back!

Here is a picture of my family...

date: _____

Today I feel...

😁 🙂 😐 🙁 😠 😛 😮 😖

I am grateful for

1. _____

2. _____

3. _____

Something that made me smile today...

_____

This is the best thing that happened to me today...

date: _____

Today I feel...

😄 🙂 😐 🙁 😠 😋 😮 😖

I am grateful for

1. _____

2. _____

3. _____

Today I learned...

_____

This is the best thing that happened to me today...

date: _____

Today I feel...

😁 🙂 😐 🙁 😣 😛 😲 😖

I am grateful for

1. _____

2. _____

3. _____

This person made me happy today...

_____

This is the best thing that happened to me today...

date: _____

Today I feel...

😄 🙂 😐 🙁 😠 😜 😮 😰

I am grateful for

1. _____

2. _____

3. _____

This is what I am looking forward to next week...

_____

This is the best thing that happened to me today...

Today I feel...

😄 🙂 😐 🙁 😠 😛 😲 😖

I am grateful for

1. _____

2. _____

3. _____

This is one nice thing I did for someone today...

_____

This is the best thing that happened to me today...

Home is where the heart is!

My favorite place in my home to spend time is...

_____

This is what that space looks like and what I like to do there...

Today I feel...

😁 🙂 😐 🙁 😠 😛 😮 😣

I am grateful for

1. _____

2. _____

3. _____

Something that made me smile today...

_____

This is the best thing that happened to me today...

date: _____

Today I feel...

😁 🙂 😐 🙁 😠 😋 😮 😖

I am grateful for

1. _____

2. _____

3. _____

Today I learned...

_____

This is the best thing that happened to me today...

Today I feel...

😄 🙂 😐 🙁 😠 😝 😮 😖

I am grateful for

1. _____

2. _____

3. _____

This person made me happy today...

_____

This is the best thing that happened to me today...

date: _____

Today I feel...

😁 🙂 😐 🙁 😠 😝 😮 😰

I am grateful for

1. _____

2. _____

3. _____

This is what I am looking forward to next week...

_____

This is the best thing that happened to me today...

date: _____

Today I feel...

😄 🙂 😐 🙁 😠 😛 😲 😖

I am grateful for

1. _____

2. _____

3. _____

This is one nice thing I did for someone today...

_____

This is the best thing that happened to me today...

Beautiful as all seaons!

What I love the most about Spring...

What I love the most about Summer...

What I love the most about Fall...

What I love the most about Winter...

date: _____

Today I feel...

😀 🙂 😐 🙁 😠 😛 😮 😣

I am grateful for

1. _____

2. _____

3. _____

Something that made me smile today...

_____

This is the best thing that happened to me today...

date: _____

Today I feel...

😁 🙂 😐 🙁 😠 😜 😮 😖

I am grateful for

1. _____

2. _____

3. _____

Today I learned...

_____

This is the best thing that happened to me today...

date: _____

Today I feel...

😁 🙂 😐 🙁 😠 😝 😮 😖

I am grateful for

1. _____

2. _____

3. _____

This person made me happy today...

_____

This is the best thing that happened to me today...

date: _____

Today I feel...

😁 🙂 😐 🙁 😠 😛 😮 😟

I am grateful for

1. _____

2. _____

3. _____

This is what I am looking forward to next week...

_____

This is the best thing that happened to me today...

date: _____

Today I feel...

😄 🙂 😐 🙁 😠 😝 😮 😖

I am grateful for

1. _____

2. _____

3. _____

This is one nice thing I did for someone today...

_____

This is the best thing that happened to me today...

I love to celebrate with my friends and family!

My favorite holiday is...

_____

This is what I love to do and who I like to spend my time with during this holiday...

Today I feel...

😁 🙂 😐 ☹️ 😠 😜 😮 😖

I am grateful for

1. _____

2. _____

3. _____

Something that made me smile today...

_____

This is the best thing that happened to me today...

date: _____

Today I feel...

😄 🙂 😐 🙁 😠 😛 😮 😖

I am grateful for

1. _____

2. _____

3. _____

Today I learned...

_____

This is the best thing that happened to me today...

date: _____

Today I feel...

😆 🙂 😐 🙁 😠 😛 😮 😖

I am grateful for

1. _____

2. _____

3. _____

This person made me happy today...

_____

This is the best thing that happened to me today...

Today I feel...

😆 🙂 😐 🙁 😠 😛 😮 😣

I am grateful for

1. _____

2. _____

3. _____

This is what I am looking forward to next week...

_____

This is the best thing that happened to me today...

date: _____

Today I feel...

😁 😊 😐 🙁 😠 😝 😯 😖

I am grateful for

1. _____

2. _____

3. _____

This is one nice thing I did for someone today...

_____

This is the best thing that happened to me today...

Have big dreams.
You will grow into them!

One of my many big dreams is to...

_____

This is my dream or me living my dream...

Today I feel...

😄 🙂 😐 🙁 😠 😛 😮 😖

I am grateful for

1. _____

2. _____

3. _____

Something that made me smile today...

_____

This is the best thing that happened to me today...

date: _____

Today I feel...

😁 🙂 😐 🙁 😠 😋 😮 😖

I am grateful for

1. _____

2. _____

3. _____

Today I learned...

_____

This is the best thing that happened to me today...

date: _____

Today I feel...

😁　🙂　😐　🙁　😠　😛　😮　😖

I am grateful for

1. _____

2. _____

3. _____

This person made me happy today...

_____

This is the best thing that happened to me today...

Today I feel...

😄 🙂 😐 🙁 😠 😛 😮 😣

I am grateful for

1. _____

2. _____

3. _____

This is what I am looking forward to next week...

_____

This is the best thing that happened to me today...

date: _____

Today I feel...

😁 🙂 😐 🙁 😠 😝 😮 😖

I am grateful for

1. _____

2. _____

3. _____

This is one nice thing I did for someone today...

_____

This is the best thing that happened to me today...

I can say "Thank You" in 10 Languages!

French
merci
"mehr-see"

German
danke
"dang-ke"

Arabic
shukran
"shoo-kran"

Hindi
shukriya
"shook-dee-ah"

Afrikaans
dankie
"don kee"

Spanish
gracias
"grah-syahs"

Italian
grazie
"graht-tsyeh"

Portuguese
obrigado
"oh-bree-gah-doo"

Russian
спасибо
"spuh-see-buh"

Japanese
arigatô
"ah-ree-gah-toh"

date: _____

Today I feel...

😄 🙂 😐 🙁 😠 😝 😲 😟

I am grateful for

1. _____

2. _____

3. _____

Something that made me smile today...

_____

This is the best thing that happened to me today...

date: _____

Today I feel...

😄 🙂 😐 🙁 😠 😝 😲 😟

I am grateful for

1. _____

2. _____

3. _____

Today I learned...

_____

This is the best thing that happened to me today...

date: _____

Today I feel...

😁 🙂 😐 🙁 😠 😛 😮 😖

I am grateful for

1. _____

2. _____

3. _____

This person made me happy today...

_____

This is the best thing that happened to me today...

date: _____

Today I feel...

😄 🙂 😐 🙁 😠 😛 😮 😖

I am grateful for

1. _____

2. _____

3. _____

This is what I am looking forward to next week...

_____

This is the best thing that happened to me today...

date: _____

Today I feel...

😆 🙂 😐 🙁 😠 😝 😮 😖

I am grateful for

1. _____

2. _____

3. _____

This is one nice thing I did for someone today...

_____

This is the best thing that happened to me today...

Friends are the sunshine of life!

One of my best friends is _____

I met my friend at _____

I am thankful for my friend because...

_____

My favorite thing to do with my friend is...

_____

This is a drawing of my friend and me playing our favorite thing...

date: _____

Today I feel...

😁 🙂 😐 🙁 😠 😜 😮 😖

I am grateful for

1. _____

2. _____

3. _____

Something that made me smile today...

_____

This is the best thing that happened to me today...

date: _____

Today I feel...

😁 🙂 😐 🙁 😠 😛 😮 😟

I am grateful for

1. _____

2. _____

3. _____

Today I learned...

_____

This is the best thing that happened to me today...

date: _____

Today I feel...

😄 🙂 😐 🙁 😠 😛 😮 😖

I am grateful for

1. _____

2. _____

3. _____

This person made me happy today...

_____

This is the best thing that happened to me today...

date: _____

Today I feel...

😁 🙂 😐 🙁 😠 😜 😲 😖

I am grateful for

1. _____

2. _____

3. _____

This is what I am looking forward to next week...

_____

This is the best thing that happened to me today...

date: _____

Today I feel...

😁 🙂 😐 🙁 😠 😛 😮 😖

I am grateful for

1. _____

2. _____

3. _____

This is one nice thing I did for someone today...

_____

This is the best thing that happened to me today...

I am a rockstar!

These are talents or skills of which I am most proud.

1. _____

2. _____

3. _____

This is a drawing of me doing one of these things...

Today I feel...

😄 🙂 😐 🙁 😠 😝 😯 😖

I am grateful for

1. _____

2. _____

3. _____

Something that made me smile today...

_____

This is the best thing that happened to me today...

Today I feel...

😄 🙂 😐 🙁 😠 😛 😮 😖

I am grateful for

1. _____

2. _____

3. _____

Today I learned...

_____

This is the best thing that happened to me today...

date: _____

Today I feel...

😁 🙂 😐 🙁 😠 😛 😮 😖

I am grateful for

1. _____

2. _____

3. _____

This person made me happy today...

_____

This is the best thing that happened to me today...

date: _____

Today I feel...

😁 🙂 😐 🙁 😣 😝 😲 😖

I am grateful for

1. _____

2. _____

3. _____

This is what I am looking forward to next week...

_____

This is the best thing that happened to me today...

Today I feel...

😁 😊 😐 🙁 😣 😛 😮 😖

I am grateful for

1. _____

2. _____

3. _____

This is one nice thing I did for someone today...

_____

This is the best thing that happened to me today...

I love to learn and grow!

My favorite teacher is _____

This teacher is my favorite because...

_____

My favorite subject is _____

and I love to learn about _____

This is a picture of me enjoying my favorite thing
about school...

date: _____

Today I feel...

😁 😊 😐 🙁 😠 😛 😮 😖

I am grateful for

1. _____

2. _____

3. _____

Something that made me smile today...

_____

This is the best thing that happened to me today...

date: _____

Today I feel...

😁 🙂 😐 🙁 😣 😜 😮 😖

I am grateful for

1. _____

2. _____

3. _____

Today I learned...

_____

This is the best thing that happened to me today...

date: _____

Today I feel...

😁 🙂 😐 🙁 😠 😝 😮 😖

I am grateful for

1. _____

2. _____

3. _____

This person made me happy today...

_____

This is the best thing that happened to me today...

Today I feel...

😄 🙂 😐 🙁 😠 😛 😮 😖

I am grateful for

1. _____

2. _____

3. _____

This is what I am looking forward to next week...

_____

This is the best thing that happened to me today...

Today I feel...

😁 🙂 😐 🙁 😠 😛 😮 😟

I am grateful for

1. _____

2. _____

3. _____

This is one nice thing I did for someone today...

_____

This is the best thing that happened to me today...

Thank You - two words that can brighten someone elses day!

Recently I recieved a gift from someone. This is a thank you note I made for them. I can cut it out and give it to them.

Thank You - two words that can brighten someone elses day!

Recently I recieved a gift from someone. This is a thank you note I made for them. I can cut it out and give it to them.

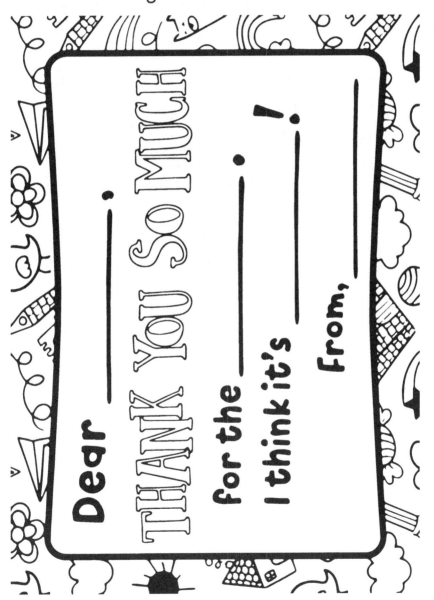

Thank You - two words that can brighten someone elses day!

Recently I recieved a gift from someone. This is a thank you note I made for them. I can cut it out and give it to them.

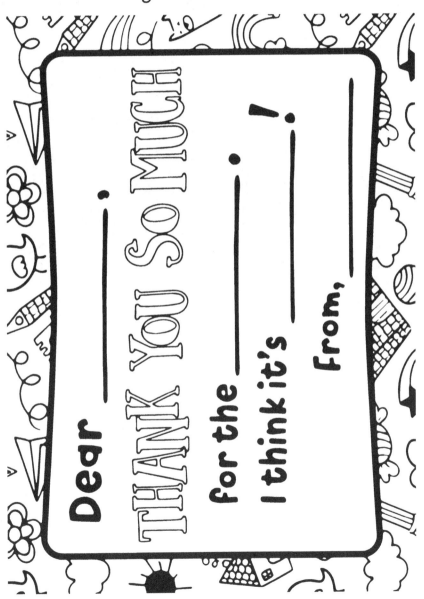

Thank You - two words that can brighten someone elses day!

Recently I recieved a gift from someone. This is a thank you note I made for them. I can cut it out and give it to them.

Thank You - two words that can brighten someone elses day!

Recently I recieved a gift from someone. This is a thank you note I made for them. I can cut it out and give it to them.

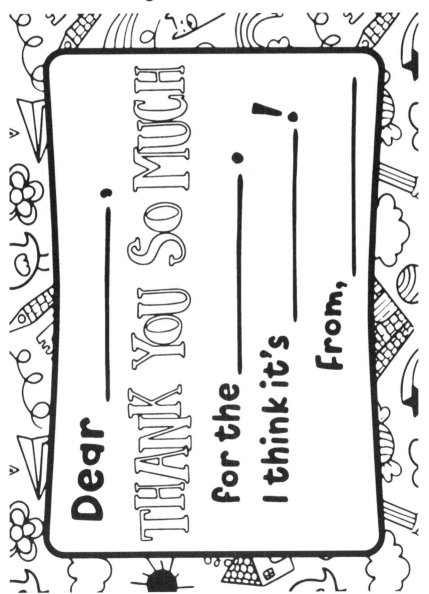

Drake Mason

hello@drakemason.com

Made in the USA
Coppell, TX
06 December 2020